All you need to know about Denmark

Copyright © 2023 Jonas Hoffmann-Schmidt.
Translation: Linda Amber Chambers.

All rights reserved. This book, including all its parts, is protected by copyright. Any use outside the narrow limits of copyright law is prohibited without the written consent of the author. This book has been created using artificial intelligence to provide unique and informative content.

Disclaimer: This book is for entertainment purposes only. The information, facts and views contained therein have been researched and compiled to the best of our knowledge and belief. Nevertheless, the author and the publisher assume no liability for the accuracy or completeness of the information. Readers should consult with professionals before making any decisions based on this information. Use of this book is the responsibility of the reader.

Introduction: The fascination of Denmark 6

Geography and landscape 9

Denmark's turbulent history: from the Vikings to modern times 12

The Viking Period: Conquests and Trade 15

The Kalmar Union: Denmark's link to Sweden and Norway 18

The Renaissance and Denmark's cultural heyday 20

The Introduction of the Constitutional Monarchy 23

Denmark in the 19th Century: Wars and Political Changes 25

The Golden Age of Danish Literature and Art 28

Denmark in the 20th Century: World Wars and Social Developments 31

Today's modern Danish society 34

Denmark's stunning wildlife 37

National Parks and Nature Reserves 39

Denmark's unique cuisine: from Smørrebrød to Rødgrød med Fløde 41

New Nordic cuisine: Denmark's contribution to global gastronomy 43

Copenhagen: A journey through the capital 45

Aarhus: history, culture and lifestyle 48

Odense: Auf den Spuren Hans Christian Andersens 51

Aalborg: Modern developments in a historic city 53

Roskilde: Culture and history of the old Viking town 56

Denmark's maritime traditions and fishing villages 59

Kronborg Castle: Shakespeare's Hamlet and Danish History 62

Legoland Billund: A World of Colorful Building Blocks 64

Tivoli Gardens: Entertainment and magic at Copenhagen's theme park 67

The Royal Castles of Denmark 70

Denmark's contribution to the music world: from classical music to pop 73

Hygge: The secret to Danish well-being 79

The Art of Danish Craftsmanship: Glassblowing and Ceramics 82

The importance of cycling in Denmark 85

Denmark's folk festivals and traditions 88

The Danish language: history and characteristics 91

Cultural Politeness and Etiquette 94

The role of religion in Danish society 96

Educational system and intellectual traditions 99

Denmark's social welfare policy 102

Sustainability and environmental protection in Denmark 105

Denmark's role in the EU and international relations 108

Art Galleries and Museums: Preserving Denmark's Cultural Heritage 111

A look into the future: challenges and opportunities for Denmark 114

Epilogue 116

Introduction: The fascination of Denmark

Welcome to a captivating journey of discovery through the enchanting country of Denmark. Proud of its rich history, stunning nature, and unique culture, this Nordic nation invites you to explore its facets and understand what makes it so fascinating.

From picturesque coastlines to lush forests and vibrant cities, Denmark is a land of contrasts and diversity. It is the birthplace of great writers such as Hans Christian Andersen and offers a rich cultural scene ranging from classical music to modern design. This introduction will provide you with an overview of some of the most fascinating aspects that will be explored in detail in the coming chapters.

Denmark's history dates back to Viking times, when brave sailors crossed the seas and made the country a center of trade and conquest. The traces of this era can still be felt in the country's historical sites and cultural identity. The Kalmar Union brought Denmark together with Sweden and Norway and shaped the political landscape of the time.

The Renaissance brought about a cultural heyday in which Denmark played a leading role in art, literature and science. Later, the country underwent political changes when the constitutional monarchy was introduced and Denmark adopted a modern form of government. The 19th century brought wars and territorial losses, but Denmark overcame these challenges and developed into a modern society.

Denmark's wildlife is as fascinating as the country's history. National parks and nature reserves provide habitat for a wide variety of animals, from red deer to white-tailed eagles. Denmark's unique cuisine, ranging from hearty dishes like Smørrebrød to delicious desserts like Rødgrød med Fløde, reflects the country's connection to nature and agriculture.

Denmark's cities tell stories of tradition and modernity. Copenhagen, the capital, is an urban center with royal flair and cultural richness. Aarhus, Odense, Aalborg and Roskilde each contribute to the fascinating diversity of Danish cities.

Denmark's cultural aspects extend to music, handicrafts, design and traditions. The Danes have a unique concept of "hygge" that embodies cosiness and well-being. The Danish language itself has a fascinating history and features that show its connection to the country's history.

Immerse yourself in the fascination of Denmark as we delve into these aspects and many more in the following chapters. A journey through the rich past, diverse nature and impressive culture of this country awaits you.

Geography and landscape

Denmark, the country located between the North Sea and the Baltic Sea, impresses with its multifaceted geography and picturesque landscape. Its location in the north of Europe makes it a unique place, shaped by the influences of the sea and nature. The coastline stretches for more than 7,300 kilometres, forming an important feature of the Danish identity.

The western coast of Denmark, along the North Sea, is characterized by wide sandy beaches and impressive dune landscapes. Here, rough winds crash against the land, while the waves of the North Sea water crash against the shores. This region is popular with surfers and nature lovers alike and offers spectacular sunsets over the sea.

The eastern coast of the country, which runs along the Baltic Sea, presents a softer and calmer scenery. Here you will find picturesque fishing villages, marinas and historic towns. The Baltic Sea is known for its clear waters, which offer opportunities for sailing, swimming and fishing. The islands off the east coast, including Zealand, Funen and Lolland, are rich in history and nature.

The Danish mainland is characterized by flat plains, hilly landscapes and fertile fields. The North German Plain stretches across the western part of Denmark and is an important agricultural area. The landscape is crisscrossed by numerous rivers that flow into the surrounding seas.

A notable geographical feature of Denmark is the fjords that stretch along the west coast. A legacy of the last ice age, these deep, winding waterways offer a spectacular sight surrounded by cliffs and verdant slopes.

Denmark is also known for its numerous lakes, which are spread throughout the country. The largest lake, the Little Belt, stretches between Jutland and Funen. Not only do these bodies of water provide a picturesque backdrop, but they also serve as important habitats for various species of animals.

The Danish landscape is also characterized by forests, which make up about 15% of the country's total area. These forests not only provide recreational opportunities for the population, but are also home to a variety of animal and plant species. These include red deer, foxes, badgers and various species of birds.

Overall, Denmark's geography reflects the country's close connection to nature. The varied landscape, from the rugged North Sea coast to the rolling hills of the mainland, offers a variety of experiences for locals and visitors alike.

Denmark's turbulent history: from the Vikings to modern times

The history of Denmark is a captivating chapter in European development, spanning from the early days of the Vikings to today's modern society. The roots of this country go back to a time when brave seafarers crossed the seas and roamed the Nordic coasts with their dragon ships.

The Viking era, which began in the 8th century, marks a turning point in Denmark's history. These seafaring warriors and explorers were known for their conquests and trading ventures, which took them as far away as England, Ireland, and other parts of Europe. Their presence left their mark not only on the history books, but also on the culture and legends of the time.

In the 10th century, Denmark began to establish itself as a political power, and the famous Danish kings such as Harald Bluetooth and Knut the Great shaped the country's fortunes. Under the reign of Knut, the Danish Empire stretched across parts of

England, Norway and Sweden. The cultural and economic ties forged during this period have left their mark on the country.

The Kalmar Union, founded in the 14th century, united Denmark with Sweden and Norway in a single political entity. This union, led by common kings, was intended to bring the regions closer together, but it also led to tensions and conflicts. The union lasted until the 16th century, when the countries broke away from each other again.

The Renaissance brought a cultural heyday to Denmark known as the "Golden Age". King Christian IV promoted art, science and architecture and left behind a legacy of magnificent castles and buildings. Denmark became a center of humanism and enlightenment in Northern Europe.

In the 19th century, Denmark was shaken by political changes and wars. The loss of Norway and Schleswig led to territorial losses, but the country continued on its path to modernization. The introduction of the constitutional monarchy in 1849 laid the foundation for Denmark's modern political system.

The 20th century brought both highs and lows for Denmark. During the two world wars, the country remained neutral, but it experienced social and economic challenges. In the post-war period, Denmark evolved into a modern welfare society with a strong emphasis on social security, education, and health care.

Today's modern society in Denmark is characterized by progress, innovation and international cooperation. The country plays an active role in the European Union and is known for its sustainable initiatives, design culture and high quality of life.

Denmark's eventful history is a reflection of the changes and developments in Europe. From the Vikings, through the times of the Reformation, wars and political upheavals, to today's cosmopolitan and progressive nation, Denmark is a country that wears its past with pride while welcoming the future with openness.

The Viking Period: Conquests and Trade

The Viking era, which began in the 8th century and lasted until the 11th century, marked a dramatic period in the history of Denmark and the entire Nordic region. These seafaring adventurers and warriors, known as Vikings, not only left their mark on the Nordic coasts, but also left an indelible mark on the history books and culture of the time.

The Vikings came from Denmark, Norway and Sweden and were known for their characteristic dragon ships, which they used to cross the seas and reach far-flung lands. Their travels took them west towards England and Ireland, but also east to the Baltic region and Russia. The impressive shipping technology of the Vikings allowed them to explore unknown coasts and rivers and open up new trade routes.

Conquests were an important aspect of Viking life. They carried out raids on coastal towns and villages to make booty and establish trade contacts. These raids, though often violent, also served the exchange of goods, culture, and ideas. The Vikings established settlements in distant lands such as Iceland, Greenland, and even North America, as evidenced by the discovery of remains at L'Anse aux Meadows.

A notable event from this period was the discovery and settlement of Iceland. The Vikings reached the island in the 9th century and established settlements there. Iceland became not only a center for trade, but also for the development of Old Norse literature and jurisprudence. The famous Icelandic sagas, epic tales of heroes and gods, are a legacy of this period.

Denmark itself was an important center of Viking culture. Places like Jelling, with its monumental runestones, are witnesses to the political power and legacy of that era. The legendary King Harald Bluetooth played a crucial role in the Christianization of Denmark and influenced the consolidation of the country.

However, trade was just as important as the conquests for the Vikings. They were skilled traders who brought goods such as wood, furs, metals, and slaves to distant regions and in return brought back exotic goods such as spices, gemstones, and silk. Denmark and other Nordic countries became important hubs in the trade routes of the Middle Ages.

The time of the Vikings was characterized by a thirst for adventure, discovery and cultural exchange. Not only have they shaped the Nordic countries, but they have also influenced the history of Europe and beyond. The Vikings left behind a rich heritage of stories, artifacts, and traditions that are still alive today, passing on their fascination for generations to come.

The Kalmar Union: Denmark's link to Sweden and Norway

The era of the Kalmar Union, which began in the 14th century and lasted until the 16th century, represents an important period in Denmark's history. This union, which linked Denmark with Sweden and Norway, led to political changes, tensions and challenges that shaped the political face of Northern Europe.

The Kalmar Union was established in 1397 by the election of Queen Margaret I of Denmark, also known as Margaret of Valdemar, as Queen of Norway, Sweden and Denmark. This union was intended to unite the three countries under a common ruler and thus ensure political stability in the region.

However, the Kalmar Union was not always one of harmony. Despite the common ruler, the three countries retained a certain autonomy and their own interests. This led to tensions and conflicts, especially between Denmark and Sweden. The political landscape was marked by intrigues, power games and rival interests of the noble houses.

During the Kalmar Union, Denmark sought to consolidate its position as the dominant power within the Union. However, King Christian II of Denmark led a repressive rule that led to unrest in Sweden. This discontent ultimately led to Sweden's secession from the Union in 1523, when Gustav I Vasa ascended the Swedish throne and declared independence.

The Kalmar Union thus ended in 1523, after more than 100 years of political integration between the Nordic countries. While the Union did not achieve the desired goal of political stability, it nevertheless left a lasting mark on the history and culture of these countries. Relations between Denmark, Sweden and Norway were shaped by this era and continue to influence regional cooperation and connection to this day.

The Kalmar Union illustrates the complex challenges involved in trying to unite different countries and interests. Although it did not last, it has shaped the history of the Nordic region and is a significant chapter in the development of Denmark and its relations with its neighbours.

The Renaissance and Denmark's cultural heyday

The Renaissance period, which began in the 15th century and lasted until the 17th century, marked a remarkable period of cultural awakening in Europe. In Denmark, this period manifested itself as an era of creative flourishing and intellectual progress. While the Renaissance began primarily in Italy, its appeal spread across the continent, and Denmark was no exception.

Under the reign of King Christian IV, who reigned from 1588 to 1648, Denmark experienced a period of extraordinary cultural activity. Christian IV promoted the arts, architecture and sciences and left behind a rich legacy of magnificent buildings that shape the cityscape of Copenhagen today. Under his reign, castles such as the famous Rosenborg Slot and the imposing Kronborg Castle were built.

The Renaissance in Denmark was also reflected in literature and music. Danish humanism, promoted by scholars such as Peder Laale and Anders Sørensen Vedel, emphasized the rediscovery of classical works and the spread of education. Old Norse literature was revived, and the translation of the Edda contributed to the preservation of cultural heritage.

Music, meanwhile, flourished with the founding of the Royal Chapel by King Christian IV and the promotion of composers such as Mogens Pedersøn and Heinrich Schütz. This musical renaissance contributed to the development of a unique Danish musical tradition that continues to this day.

A prominent figure of this period was the astronomer Tycho Brahe, known for his groundbreaking contributions to astronomy. Brahe's close observations of the celestial bodies laid the foundation for later scientific discoveries and had a lasting impact on the understanding of the universe.

However, Denmark's cultural heyday during the Renaissance also had its downsides. Despite the cultural boom, the country struggled with financial challenges and political unrest. Efforts to achieve religious unity and the increasing political influence of neighboring countries such as Sweden and Germany had an impact on the stability of the kingdom.

The Renaissance in Denmark was marked by a diverse range of cultural, intellectual and artistic achievements. It produced not only impressive buildings and works of art, but also a spirit of research and education that laid the foundation for later developments. The cultural heyday of the Renaissance continues to shape Denmark's cultural heritage and is a testament to the country's ability to thrive creatively in times of change and challenges.

The Introduction of the Constitutional Monarchy

The introduction of the constitutional monarchy in Denmark marked a decisive step in the country's political evolution. This significant era, which began in the 19th century, led to profound changes in Denmark's power structure and form of government. The constitutional monarchy paved the way for a more modern, democratic society and laid the foundation for the political landscape we know today.

The conditions for the introduction of constitutional monarchy were created by a combination of internal and external factors. The decline of absolute monarchy and the influence of the Enlightenment in Europe led to a growing need for political participation and freedoms. The French Revolution and the ideals of human rights and equality also inspired reform movements in Denmark.

The political situation in Denmark was further shaken by the war with Great Britain and the subsequent Napoleonic Continental Blockade. These events led to economic difficulties and discontent among the population. The need for political change to stabilize and move the country forward became increasingly apparent.

In 1849, King Frederik VII of Denmark signed the constitution that introduced the constitutional monarchy. The constitution established a parliamentary form of government and created a bicameral system consisting of the Landsting (upper house) and the Folketing (lower house). The king's power was limited in favor of an elected parliament, resulting in a more balanced distribution of political power.

The introduction of the constitutional monarchy led to a strengthening of civil rights and freedoms. Freedom of expression, freedom of the press and the right to political participation were protected and promoted. This allowed for a lively political debate and fostered the development of a democratic culture in Denmark. The constitutional monarchy also led to social reforms and economic progress. Education and social security were expanded, and the country developed into a modern welfare society. Denmark has been internationally recognized for its progressive policies and efforts to achieve social justice.

The introduction of the constitutional monarchy was thus a turning point in Denmark's history, setting the country on the path to democracy and modernization. This era has left a lasting mark on Denmark's political landscape and core values, and is an example of how a country is facing the challenges of its time and finding a path to a better future.

Denmark in the 19th Century: Wars and Political Changes

The 19th century was an era of turbulence, political challenges and profound changes for Denmark. During this period, the country faced a series of wars, territorial losses and political upheavals that left a lasting mark on its history.

The Napoleonic Wars, which shook Europe during the late 18th and early 19th centuries, also had an impact on Denmark. The Napoleonic Continental Blockade, imposed by Napoleon Bonaparte, led to economic difficulties for the Danish kingdom. The British fleet attacked Denmark in 1801 and 1807 to weaken the Danish navy and take control of the Danish fleet squadrons.

A pivotal moment in Denmark's history was the loss of Norway in 1814 as a result of the Kiel Peace Treaty. Due to the political changes in Europe, Denmark had to cede Norway to Sweden. This loss had an impact not only on the territory, but also on Denmark's national identity and self-image.

Domestically, the 19th century was marked by efforts for political change and reforms. The desire for more civil rights, political participation and freedom of expression increased. Over the course of the century, steps were taken towards a constitutional monarchy, which was finally realized in 1849 with the adoption of a constitution.

The Schleswig-Holstein question posed a further challenge for Denmark. The duchies of Schleswig and Holstein, which belonged to Denmark, were also connected to the German Confederation. The Danish government's efforts to strengthen the integration of these duchies into the Danish Kingdom led to tensions with the German Confederation and ultimately to the German-Danish War of 1864. Denmark suffered a crushing defeat and had to cede Schleswig, Holstein and Lauenburg to Prussia and Austria.

These territorial losses had a profound impact on Danish society and politics. The loss of territories and the political setbacks led to a national identity crisis and intensified the desire for political change. The subsequent reforms and the introduction of the constitutional monarchy in 1849 helped stabilize the political landscape and lay the foundations for a more modern society.

The 19th century was a time of trials and challenges for Denmark. Wars, territorial losses and political upheavals shaped the country's history and laid the foundation for its further development in the 20th century. Despite the difficulties, Denmark showed a remarkable ability to adapt to the changes and find its way to a modern society.

The Golden Age of Danish Literature and Art

The 19th century marked a cultural and artistic flourishing for Denmark, often known as the "Golden Age". During this period, Danish literature, art and culture reached extraordinary heights that put the country on the international stage and exerted a lasting influence on national identity.

The period of the Golden Age was marked by a deep engagement with national identity and cultural heritage. It was during this period that Denmark sought its roots and developed a strong attachment to Old Norse literature and history. The Edda and the Sagas were rediscovered and reinterpreted, and Danish literature began to draw inspiration from the Romantic movement.

Notable Danish writers such as Hans Christian Andersen and Søren Kierkegaard were important figures of this era. Andersen, who is known worldwide for his fairy tales, brought about a new dimension of literature that was appealing to children and adults alike. His works, including "The Little Mermaid" and "The Ugly Duckling", have been translated into numerous languages and still have their place in the literary world today.

Søren Kierkegaard, on the other hand, was an important philosopher, theologian and writer. His writings, which dealt with questions of existence, faith and ethics, had a profound influence on philosophical development not only in Denmark but worldwide. Kierkegaard's emphasis on individual existence and subjective truth reflected the intellectual currents of the era.

Art also flourished in the Golden Age. Artists such as Christoffer Wilhelm Eckersberg and Constantin Hansen created works that depicted nature and daily life in a realistic way. These artists were part of the so-called "Copenhagen School of Painting", which had a significant influence on Danish art and beyond.

Architecture also flourished, with King Christian IV promoting the development of castles and buildings in the Renaissance style in the 17th century. The construction of the impressive Frederiksborg Palace and the ornate Rosenborg Slot are examples of this period of architectural splendour.

The golden age of Danish literature and art was marked by a deep attachment to national identity, romantic aesthetics and intellectual exploration. During this period, Denmark found a cultural voice that resonated in both literature and art, establishing the country as a major creative force on the world stage. The works and ideas of this era have shaped Denmark's national identity to this day and are a shining example of the culture's ability to thrive in challenging times.

Denmark in the 20th Century: World Wars and Social Developments

The 20th century was a time of great upheaval for Denmark, shaping the country in the midst of world wars, political changes and social developments. During this era, Denmark was drawn into the maelstrom of global events and underwent a transformation that left a lasting mark on its history.

The First World War, which raged from 1914 to 1918, also brought challenges for Denmark. Although the country remained neutral, the war had an impact on the economy and the supply situation. After the war, Denmark played an active role in the establishment of the League of Nations and participated in international efforts to promote peace and cooperation.

The interwar period brought social and political changes. The introduction of women's suffrage in 1915 was a milestone for democracy and equality in Denmark. Women gained the opportunity to become politically active and participate in the country's decision-making processes.

The Second World War, which raged from 1939 to 1945, left deep scars on Denmark. The country was occupied by Nazi Germany in 1940, which led to serious restrictions on freedom and sovereignty. However, Denmark did not remain passive during the occupation: the rescue operation to save Danish Jews from deportation to concentration camps testifies to the courage and solidarity of the Danish population.

The liberation of Denmark in 1945 marked a turning point that set the country on the path to restoring freedom and democracy. After the war, Denmark became a member of the United Nations and NATO, and the country was actively involved in the promotion of human rights and international cooperation.

The post-war period brought social reforms and the expansion of the welfare state. Denmark developed into a modern welfare society with a strong focus on education, health care and social security. The concept of "flexicurity", which involves a combination of flexible labour markets and social protection, has become a model for other countries.

The Cold War and the division of Europe also influenced Denmark's politics and security situation. However, the country continued to rely on diplomacy and international cooperation to defend its interests and contribute to stability in the region.

The 20th century was a time of trials and changes for Denmark. World wars, political developments and social reforms have shaped the country and strengthened its identity as a democratic, social and committed member of the global community. The developments of this era have laid the foundations for modern Denmark and show how a nation can grow and evolve in times of challenge.

Today's modern Danish society

Today's modern Danish society reflects the advances, values and principles that have developed over the centuries. Denmark has evolved into a modern, prosperous and inclusive society known for its social justice, education systems and quality of life.

One of the outstanding features of modern Danish society is its welfare state. The Danish welfare system, which is based on the principle of social protection, provides comprehensive health care, education, unemployment benefits and pension benefits. This system has helped to reduce social inequality and improve living conditions for all citizens.

The education system in Denmark is also remarkable. It provides free and quality education from primary school to university. The dual education system allows students to develop academic and professional skills and prepare for the job market. The emphasis on education contributes to the advancement of society and promotes a knowledge-based economy.

Gender equality is a central concern in modern Danish society. Denmark has been actively involved in promoting gender equality and is known for its progressive approaches to reconciling work and family life. Women are strongly represented in various areas of public life, politics and business.

Danish politics is characterised by consensus building and democratic participation. The multi-party system encourages discussion and compromise between political parties. Denmark is also known for its open and transparent governance, which boosts citizens' trust in the institutions.

Danish society has become multicultural and diverse. The immigration of people from different countries has enriched the cultural mosaic of the country. Denmark promotes the integration of immigrants and refugees in order to create an inclusive society characterized by diversity and mutual respect.

Environmental awareness is another hallmark of modern Danish society. Denmark has become a pioneer in renewable energy, sustainability and environmental protection. The promotion of green technologies and efforts to reduce CO_2 emissions have made the country a global role model for environmental protection.

Modern Danish society is characterized by its commitment to social justice, education, gender equality, diversity and environmental protection. It has constantly evolved from its historical roots to the present day and remains committed to being a model for an inclusive, progressive and livable society.

Denmark's stunning wildlife

Denmark's wildlife may not be as exotic as some other countries, but it has its own charm and peculiarities. The country, which is surrounded by the North Sea and the Baltic Sea, is home to a diverse range of animals that have adapted to the unique Nordic environment.

Denmark's coastline stretches for several thousand kilometres and provides an ideal habitat for many marine species. Along the beaches and rocks, seals can be seen sunbathing or playing in the water. Greylag geese and eider ducks are also common sightings on the coasts.

Danish forests and nature reserves are also home to some impressive animal species. Deer are common and are often seen in the early morning hours or at dusk. Squirrels flit between the trees, making for a lively sight. Wild boars and foxes are also part of the Danish fauna.

Denmark's waters are rich in fish and bird species. The lakes and rivers are home to a variety of fish species, including pike, zander and perch. At the birdwatching sites along the coasts, bird enthusiasts can admire a wide range of seabirds, gulls and oystercatchers.

One of the most remarkable animal species in Denmark is the white-tailed eagle. With an imposing wingspan and majestic presence, the white-tailed eagle has experienced an impressive recovery after being almost extinct. Today, lucky observers can see it gliding over the landscape.

The Danish islands are also known for their seal colonies. On some secluded beaches, curious visitors can spot grey seals and ringed seals in their natural habitat. These lovable sea creatures are an important part of the region's ecosystem.

Denmark's stunning wildlife may seem unremarkable at first, but upon closer inspection, it reveals a plethora of fascinating and diverse life forms. The adaptability of these animals to the Nordic environment and the efforts to preserve their habitats help to preserve the natural beauty and richness of Denmark's wildlife.

National Parks and Nature Reserves

Denmark is proud of its efforts to protect the natural environment and preserve habitats for plants and animals. The country has a variety of national parks and nature reserves that reflect the diversity of the country's landscapes and ecosystems.

One of the most famous national parks in Denmark is Thy National Park in the northwest of the country. Spanning dunes, heaths, and forests, this park is home to impressive wildlife, including deer, foxes, and a variety of bird species. The Wadden Sea National Park, which stretches along the west coast of Denmark, is a UNESCO World Heritage Site and an important habitat for birds and marine life.

Another notable place is Møn National Park, which includes the picturesque island of Møn. Here, visitors can admire the unique chalk cliffs and explore the diverse flora and fauna on hiking trails. Mols Bjerge National Park in eastern Jutland offers a varied landscape of hills, lakes and forests and is a paradise for outdoor enthusiasts.

The Danish nature reserves are also of great importance for the preservation of biodiversity. Rye Mose Nature Reserve, one of Denmark's oldest moorlands, is home to rare plants and is an important habitat for birds. Kongernes Nordsjælland Nature Reserve covers forests, lakes and wetlands and provides shelter for many animal species, including wild boar and red deer.

Denmark's national parks and nature reserves not only serve to preserve nature, but also offer opportunities for outdoor activities and nature experiences. Hiking, cycling, bird watching and water sports are popular activities in these protected areas. The Danish government is also committed to sustainable tourism and educational programs to promote awareness of nature conservation.

The protection and preservation of the natural environment is a high priority in Denmark, and the country's national parks and nature reserves are a living example of this. These protected areas offer not only refuges for animals and plants, but also valuable places for recreation and the experience of nature for people. They represent Denmark's commitment to nature conservation and the preservation of the country's scenic diversity.

Denmark's unique cuisine: from Smørrebrød to Rødgrød med Fløde

Danish cuisine is characterized by a mixture of traditional dishes and modern culinary trends. The diversity of Danish gastronomy reflects the country's rich history and natural resources.

An iconic Danish dish that is known worldwide is the Smørrebrød. These are open sandwiches served on a piece of rye bread. Toppings can range from smoked salmon to pickled herring and various meats. Smørrebrød are not only delicious, but also artfully decorated and reflect Danish creativity in the kitchen.

Another traditional dish is the "stegt flæsk med persillesovs", fried pork belly with parsley sauce. This hearty dish is a classic of Danish home cooking and is often served with potatoes. The Danish hot dog, known as "pølse med brød", is a popular snack and is served with a variety of toppings such as mustard, ketchup, fried onions, and tartar sauce. Danish cuisine also makes use of the country's rich marine resources. Fish and seafood are an integral part of many dishes. The "frikadeller", a Danish meatball dish, can also be prepared with fish and is often served with tartar sauce. The "Stjerneskud" (shooting star) is a dish of fried and poached fish decorated with prawns and caviar.

The desserts of Danish cuisine are just as varied and tempting. "Æbleskiver" are small, round pancakes that are often served with powdered sugar and jam. "Rødgrød med Fløde" is a dessert made from red berries served with cream and is a delicious combination of sweet and sour. Danish cuisine has also seen a trend towards modern and innovative culinary approaches in recent years. Restaurants such as Noma in Copenhagen have brought Nordic cuisine to the world stage, highlighting innovative techniques such as fermentation and local ingredients.

Danish cuisine is a fascinating interplay of traditional dishes, local ingredients and creative influences. It reflects the country's identity and is a testament to the Danes' love of good food and shared meals. From the classic smørrebrød to the innovative creations of modern chefs, Danish cuisine has a lot to offer and remains an important part of the country's culture.

New Nordic cuisine: Denmark's contribution to global gastronomy

New Nordic cuisine, also known as "New Nordic Cuisine", is a culinary approach that originated in Denmark over the past few decades and has attracted worldwide attention. This movement has not only influenced Danish gastronomy, but also the way people around the world think about food and cuisine.

Launched in the 2000s, New Nordic Cuisine aimed to celebrate the rich tradition of Nordic ingredients and dishes while promoting innovative culinary approaches. A central principle of this movement is the emphasis on the use of local, seasonal and sustainable ingredients. The chefs of New Nordic Cuisine strive to reflect the best of Nordic nature in their creations.

A pioneer of this movement is the restaurant Noma in Copenhagen, which was founded by René Redzepi. Noma has brought New Nordic Cuisine to the world stage, focusing on ingredients such as moss, algae, wild herbs and fermented foods. Noma's creations are not only culinary masterpieces, but also an expression of Nordic identity and closeness to nature. New Nordic cuisine has not only changed the way Danish chefs cook, but has also influenced international cuisine. The movement has helped raise awareness of sustainable agriculture, local producers, and traditional culinary practices. Chefs from all over the world have been inspired by the philosophy of New Nordic Cuisine and have begun to implement similar approaches in their own kitchens.

The introduction of New Nordic Cuisine has established Denmark as a centre of culinary innovation. Not only does the country attract foodies from all over the world, but it also offers young chefs the opportunity to learn from experienced masters and develop their own culinary visions.

The New Nordic Cuisine has not only changed the way we cook, but also the perception of food and culture. It has shown that traditional ingredients and techniques can be integrated into modern, innovative cuisine. Denmark has made a valuable contribution to global gastronomy with this movement, showing how food can be not only a physical necessity, but also a source of creativity, cultural identity and sustainable development.

Copenhagen: A journey through the capital

The Danish capital, Copenhagen, is a fascinating mix of history, culture and modern way of life. With a rich past and a dynamic present, this city attracts visitors from all over the world and offers a diverse range of attractions and experiences.

The Royal Residence Amalienborg is an emblematic place in Copenhagen. Here, visitors can admire the magnificent palaces that are home to the Danish royal family. The Changing of the Guard in front of the castle is an impressive ceremony that takes place daily and highlights the royal presence.

The Little Mermaid, "Den lille Havfrue", is probably one of Copenhagen's most famous landmarks. The bronze statue, inspired by Hans Christian Andersen's fairy tales, attracts tourists from all over the world who have a special connection to this iconic figure.

Nyhavn, the new harbor, is a quaint waterfront neighborhood known for its colorful facades and charming canals. Here, visitors can walk along the shores, sit in cozy cafes and enjoy the maritime atmosphere. Nyhavn is also a popular starting point for boat tours of the city.

Copenhagen's Old Town, Indre By, is a historic center with narrow streets, cobblestone streets, and well-preserved buildings from centuries past. This is also where the Rundetårn, the round tower, is located, which offers an impressive view over the city.

Copenhagen also has a thriving cultural scene. The Design Museum Danmark, the National Museum and the Louisiana Museum of Modern Art are just a few of the institutions that showcase the country's art and culture. The Copenhagen Opera House, one of the most modern buildings in the city, offers world-class performances and concerts.

Another place not to be missed in Copenhagen is Tivoli Gardens. This historic amusement park opened in 1843 and features roller coasters, merry-go-rounds, and colorful attractions. Tivoli is not only a place for entertainment, but also a living piece of history.

Copenhagen's bike-friendliness is known worldwide. The city has well-developed cycle paths and numerous bike rental stations. Cycling is a popular way to explore the city and feel like a local.

Copenhagen is also famous for its gastronomic scene, especially New Nordic Cuisine. Restaurants like Noma have gained international recognition and attract foodies from all over the world. The city's markets, such as the Torvehallerne, offer a variety of fresh food and culinary delights.

The journey through Copenhagen takes visitors through a city that is proud of its history, but also always open to innovation and modernity. The combination of royal palaces, historic architecture, cultural treasures and modern lifestyle makes Copenhagen a unique destination that showcases the many facets of Denmark in an impressive way.

Aarhus: history, culture and lifestyle

The city of Aarhus, the second largest city in Denmark, is a place of great historical significance and cultural diversity. Its rich heritage dates back to the Viking Age and over the centuries has evolved into a modern and dynamic city that offers a unique blend of history, culture and lifestyle.

The history of Aarhus is closely linked to the Viking Age, and archaeological finds attest to the presence of Viking sites in the area. The Moesgaard Museum in Aarhus presents an impressive collection of artefacts and offers insights into the life of the Vikings. The city also has a rich medieval history, which can be felt in the old streets and buildings of the old town.

Modern Aarhus is a cultural hub with an abundance of museums, theatres and artistic events. The ARoS Aarhus Art Museum is one of the largest museums in Northern Europe and houses an impressive collection of modern and contemporary art. The Aarhus Concert Hall is a renowned venue for classical music and concerts.

Aarhus University, founded in 1928, has turned the city into an educational hub and attracts students from all over the world. The university also plays an important role in research and innovation and has contributed to the development of a modern knowledge economy in the region.

Aarhus Harbour, which has developed into a thriving neighbourhood, offers a lively mix of restaurants, shops and entertainment venues. The Dokk1 district is home to the largest public library in Scandinavia and is a place of encounter and exchange.

Aarhus is also known for its vibrant music scene. The SPOT Festival showcases up-and-coming musical talents from Denmark and internationally, while the NorthSide Festival brings national and international artists to the stage.

The lifestyle in Aarhus is characterized by a relaxed atmosphere and a strong connection to nature. The city is surrounded by beaches, forests and green parks that offer residents a wide range of leisure activities. The cycle paths and pedestrian zones contribute to environmentally friendly mobility and reflect the sustainable way of life.

The people of Aarhus are proud of their city and their community. Local markets, cafés and restaurants promote regional cuisine and a culture of togetherness. The Aarhus Ø district, which is committed to sustainable development, demonstrates the city's commitment to a modern and forward-looking way of life.

Aarhus is a city that knows how to combine its long history with contemporary culture and lifestyle. It represents the development of Denmark from its origins to the present day and is a meeting place between tradition and innovation, history and future.

Odense: Auf den Spuren Hans Christian Andersens

The city of Odense, Denmark's third largest city, is unmistakably associated with one of the world's most famous literary figures: Hans Christian Andersen. Born in 1805, Andersen is an outstanding Danish writer who is loved for his fairy tales and stories. Odense, his birthplace, proudly holds on to his memory and offers visitors the opportunity to immerse themselves in the world of his imagination and creativity.

The birthplace of Hans Christian Andersen, which now serves as a museum, is a popular destination for literature enthusiasts and tourists alike. The house offers insights into the writer's life, his works and his travels. The exhibitions feature original manuscripts, letters, drawings and personal objects that provide an insight into Andersen's life and thought.

The Odense Zoo, located in the immediate vicinity of the birthplace, was a place that Andersen often visited and that sparked his imagination. It is said that some of the animals in the zoo were his inspiration for characters in his stories. Today, visitors can explore the zoo and discover the connection between Andersen's creativity and wildlife.

Andersen Boulevard, a street in Odense, is lined with statues and monuments that honor the writer and his fairy tales. The statue of the "H.C. Andersen Self-Portrait" is a popular place for photos, while the "Tin Soldier" statue commemorates one of his famous stories.

The Hans Christian Andersen Museum, located in the heart of Odense, offers in-depth insights into the author's life and works. Interactive exhibitions and multimedia presentations convey the feeling of his stories and the significance of his work for literary history.

The annual Hans Christian Andersen Festivals attract visitors from all over the world. During the festival, parades, performances, workshops and readings are held that bring to life the magic of the writer's fairy tales.

The city of Odense has managed to carry the memory of Hans Christian Andersen into the modern age and keep his importance for world literature alive. The connection between the city and the writer is deep-rooted, and Odense has managed to use this relationship to create a unique and inspiring cultural experience for visitors who want to walk in the footsteps of Hans Christian Andersen.

Aalborg: Modern developments in a historic city

Aalborg, Denmark's fourth-largest city, is a remarkable example of the successful symbiosis of historical heritage and modern progress. This city, located in the north of the country, has a rich history dating back to the Middle Ages, and at the same time it has become a center of innovation and cultural diversity.

The history of Aalborg is marked by trade, shipbuilding and industrial development. The Limfjord, which crosses the city, played a significant role in trade with other Nordic countries and beyond. Over the centuries, Aalborg has developed into an important trading centre and maritime city.

The historic architecture of the city reflects this development. The medieval Aalborghus Castle, which rises on the shores of the Limfjord, is a testament to the city's early history. The streets of the old town are lined with well-preserved half-timbered houses that preserve the flair of past centuries.

In recent decades, however, Aalborg has undergone a remarkable transformation that has turned the city into a modern center for education, business, and culture. Aalborg University, founded in the 1970s, has become a renowned educational institution and plays an important role in research and innovation.

Aalborg's harbour front has been transformed in recent years and has developed into a lively neighbourhood. The waterfront is a popular place for walks, bike rides and leisure activities. Here you will find modern buildings, restaurants and entertainment venues that enrich the cityscape.

The cultural scene in Aalborg is also remarkable. The Utzon Center, named after the famous Danish architect Jørn Utzon, showcases modern architecture and design. The Nordkraft Cultural Centre offers a diverse range of cultural events, including concerts, theatre performances and film screenings.

An important event in Aalborg is the Carnival, which takes place every year in May. This colorful festival attracts thousands of visitors and features parades, concerts, and festivals. The Aalborg Opera Festival is another highlight in the city's cultural calendar.

The economic development of Aalborg is reflected in the growing number of companies and industries that have settled in the city. Technology companies, maritime industries and research institutions contribute to the city's economic growth and innovative strength.

The history of Aalborg and its modern transformation is a fascinating example of how a city can preserve its heritage while meeting the challenges and opportunities of the present. Aalborg is a place where history and progress go hand in hand, and a city that is proud of its past while shaping an exciting future.

Roskilde: Culture and history of the old Viking town

Roskilde, a picturesque town in eastern Denmark, is a place of great cultural significance and historical richness. This ancient Viking city has a rich history dating back to the Viking Age and is known for its impressive cathedral, maritime traditions and cultural heritage.

The history of Roskilde goes back over a thousand years. The city was founded by the Vikings in the 10th century and played an important role in the trade and politics of the region. In the Viking Age, Roskilde was an important port and trading centre, and remnants of this period are still visible today.

Roskilde Cathedral, a UNESCO World Heritage Site, is one of Denmark's oldest cathedrals and an iconic landmark of the city. The cathedral once served as the burial place for Danish kings and queens, and its imposing architecture and rich history attract visitors from all over the world.

The Viking Ship Museum in Roskilde is another highlight for history and culture lovers. The museum houses five faithful Viking ships found in the nearby fjord. These ships are a fascinating insight into the maritime skills and craft of the Vikings.

The annual Roskilde Festival is one of Europe's largest music festivals and attracts music enthusiasts from all over the world. Founded in the 1970s, the festival features a diverse selection of music genres and artists. It has become a platform for musical innovation, cultural exchange, and community development.

Roskilde also has a vibrant arts and culture scene. The Roskilde Museum presents the history of the city and its inhabitants in an interactive environment. The streets of the old town are lined with historic buildings, galleries, shops and cafes that create a rich cultural ambience.

Roskilde University, founded in the 1970s, is a centre for academic research and innovation. The university attaches great importance to interdisciplinary courses of study and practice-oriented learning approaches.

Roskilde's maritime tradition lives on in the annual Hafendagen, a festival that celebrates the city's importance as a port city. Here you can experience traditional boats, sailing competitions and maritime crafts.

The culture and history of Roskilde are closely intertwined and shape the city's attitude to life. From the Viking ships to the imposing cathedral, from the historic streets to the modern festivals, Roskilde offers a rich variety of experiences and insights into Denmark's past and present.

Denmark's maritime traditions and fishing villages

Denmark, surrounded by the North Sea and the Baltic Sea, has a long and rich maritime history that is deeply woven into the country's identity. The Danes' connection to the sea is reflected in their traditions, lifestyles and cultural practices. The fishing villages along the coast bear witness to this deep connection with the ocean.

Denmark's fishing villages have played an important role in the lives of coastal residents over the centuries. These picturesque villages are not only places of fishing, but also centers of community and culture. The colorful houses, the narrow streets and the smell of salt water give these villages a special charm.

Skagen, in the north of Denmark, is one of the most famous fishing villages in the country. Famous for its dramatic scenery and signature pair of yellow lighthouses, Skagen has long inspired artists and writers. In the 19th century, the creative atmosphere of the village attracted artists such as the Skagen painters, who captured the unique lighting mood and beauty of the surroundings.

Thyborøn, on the west coast of Denmark, is another fishing village that combines historical and modern elements. Here, visitors can visit the Jutland Aquarium and explore the fascinating underwater world of the North Sea. The harbour front of Thyborøn reflects the maritime activity of the region and is a popular place for walks and fishing activities.

Gilleleje, on the east coast of Denmark, is a traditional fishing village with an active harbour and a strong fishing tradition. The idyllic village offers not only a picturesque backdrop, but also fresh fish and seafood that can be enjoyed in the local restaurants.

Denmark's fishing villages are also closely linked to the preservation of the country's cultural identity and traditions. Fishing festivals, maritime folklore and customs are kept alive in these communities and passed on to the next generation. The fishing boats and nets are not only tools of fishing, but also symbols of the hard life and determination of the people who live with the tides.

However, Denmark's maritime tradition goes beyond the fishing villages. Sailing has a long history in the country, and Denmark has produced some of the best sailors in the world. Sailing regattas such as the "Færdern Race" and the "Tall Ships Races" attract participants and spectators from all over the world.

Denmark's maritime culture also extends to the modern fishing and maritime industries. Denmark is one of the leading countries in fisheries and has a strong maritime economy. The country's shipping industry is also of great importance and contributes to the international trade connection.

Denmark's fishing villages and maritime tradition are a tribute to the country's relationship with the sea. They are a reminder of how the sea has shaped the life and culture of the Danes and how this connection remains alive to this day. The quaint villages, fascinating stories and dedicated community show the strength and diversity of the maritime culture that forms the heart of Denmark.

Kronborg Castle: Shakespeare's Hamlet and Danish History

Kronborg Castle, majestically situated on the northeastern coast of Denmark, is a place of great historical significance and cultural heritage. Also known as "Hamlet's Castle", this imposing Renaissance castle has a rich history that intertwines with Shakespeare's famous drama "Hamlet" and the Danish monarchy.

The origins of Kronborg Castle date back to the 15th century, when King Erik VII began building a fortress to control the strategically important Öresund Strait. Over the centuries, the castle was expanded and rebuilt, and it developed into an impressive fortress with mighty walls and towers.

One of Kronborg Castle's best-known links to cultural history is the role it plays in Shakespeare's tragedy "Hamlet". Although Shakespeare never personally visited Denmark, he chose Kronborg as the setting for his drama, which is based on the old saga of the Danish prince Hamlet. The castle itself is referred to as "Elsinore" in the play, and the characters and intrigues of "Hamlet" have inextricably linked

Kronborg Castle to the literary canon. Considered one of the largest Renaissance halls in Northern Europe, the impressive ballroom of Kronborg Palace is a pinnacle of architecture and art in Denmark. The ornate ceilings and walls, as well as the magnificent paintings, convey a sense of royal pomp and historical significance.

Over the centuries, Kronborg Castle has been the scene of important events in Danish history. Kings and queens have held court here, and the castle played a role in the country's political and diplomatic affairs. In the 17th century, the castle was occupied by the Swedes during the Swedish-Danish War and later restored by King Christian IV.

Today, Kronborg Castle is a UNESCO World Heritage Site and a major tourist attraction. Visitors can explore the magnificent interiors, enjoy the impressive views of the sea, and discover the castle's rich history. Cultural events such as concerts, theatre performances and festivals are also held here every year.

Kronborg Castle is a living testimony to Danish history, culture and literature. It combines the past with the present and attracts visitors from all over the world who want to experience the historical significance, cultural beauty and literary connection of this extraordinary place.

Legoland Billund: A World of Colorful Building Blocks

Legoland Billund, the first Legoland in the world, is a place of imagination, creativity and entertainment for young and old. This colorful theme park destination in Denmark pays homage to the famous Lego bricks that have fascinated generations of children and adults for decades.

The park was opened in 1968 by Ole Kirk Christiansen, the founder of Lego, and has since become one of the most popular tourist destinations in Denmark. Legoland Billund is not only a place of leisure, but also a place of education and inspiration. The many detailed miniature landscapes and models are impressive examples of engineering and creativity.

The park includes a variety of themed areas, including "Miniland," where famous landmarks and cities are recreated from Lego. Here, visitors can travel from the Statue of Liberty to the Eiffel Tower, and the miniature models are amazingly realistic and detailed.

The attractions of Legoland Billund offer a wide range of experiences. From roller coasters and water slides to interactive rides and shows, there's something for everyone. The "Flying Eagle" offers spectacular views over the park, while the "Pirate Splash Battle" offers a wet and exciting ride through a pirate world.

The attention to detail and dedication to replicating real-world scenarios is evident in Legoland Billund. The models are not only aesthetically pleasing, but also technically impressive. The movements, sounds, and visual effects in the rides and attractions add a vivid dimension to the experience.

For young visitors, there are special areas such as "Duplo Land", which are designed to meet the needs of children and ensure that even the youngest visitors have fun. The numerous playgrounds, interactive zones and shows offer opportunities for active participation and creative play.

Legoland Billund is not only a place of entertainment, but also a place of learning. Workshops where children can learn how to create their own Lego creations encourage creativity and skills in construction. The emphasis on education and play gives the park a unique dimension that goes far beyond traditional theme parks.

The success of Legoland Billund has led to the creation of Legoland parks around the world, and the concept has gained a wide following. The combination of fun, creative development and cultural exchange has made Legoland Billund a place that captures the hearts of people of all ages, creating a world of colorful building blocks that captures the imagination and creates memories for eternity.

Tivoli Gardens: Entertainment and magic at Copenhagen's theme park

Tivoli Gardens, located in the heart of Copenhagen, is one of the oldest amusement parks in the world and a place that combines entertainment, beauty and magic. Since its opening in 1843, Tivoli has attracted millions of visitors from all over the world and has become a symbol of Danish culture and leisure.

The park was founded by Georg Carstensen and has been a place of diversity and experience from the very beginning. The mix of botanical gardens, concert stages, rides, and restaurants made Tivoli Gardens a place that caters to people of all ages and tastes. The green oases, the colorful flower beds and the well-kept landscape contribute to the relaxed atmosphere of the park.

Tivoli Gardens is famous for its classical architecture and its enchanting lighting, which transforms the park into a fairytale land at night. The famous wooden roller coaster "Rutschebanen", which has been in operation since 1914, is a popular landmark of the park and gives it a nostalgic touch. The meticulously restored rides from yesteryear, such as the 1914 "Dæmonen" carousel, are living history books of amusement park culture.

The cultural significance of Tivoli Gardens is evident in the many concerts, theatrical performances and events that have taken place over the years. The open-air concerts in the summer and the annual Christmas markets attract visitors from near and far. Artists such as Hans Christian Andersen and Walt Disney have been inspired by the magic of Tivoli Gardens.

The gastronomic offer of Tivoli Gardens is another highlight. The restaurants and cafes offer a variety of dining experiences, from Danish cuisine to international specialties. The Nimb Hotel, a historic building in the park, is known for its excellent cuisine and luxurious atmosphere.

The roller coasters and rides at Tivoli Gardens offer excitement and thrills for the adventurous. From the roller coaster "Demonen" to the interactive ghost train "Den Flyvende Kuffert" to children's attractions such as "Det Lille Tog", there is a wide range of options for all tastes.

The unique blend of history, culture and entertainment has made Tivoli Gardens a landmark that enriches and enriches Copenhagen. The park is a place where people come together to celebrate the joys of life, whether it's a leisurely stroll, a thrilling ride, or an impressive concert. Tivoli Gardens is not just an amusement park, but a place of memories, emotions and shared experiences that has been spreading joy and magic for generations.

The Royal Castles of Denmark

Denmark is rich in royal history, which is reflected in the country's magnificent royal castles. Scattered throughout the country, these impressive residences tell of Denmark's royal tradition, cultural heritage and turbulent history.

Amalienborg Palace, in the heart of Copenhagen, is the official residence of the Danish monarchy. The complex consists of four identical palaces surrounding a rectangular courtyard. Each palace represents one of the four members of the royal family: Queen Margrethe II, Crown Prince Frederik, Crown Princess Mary and Prince Joachim. The daily Changing of the Guard in front of the castle is a popular attraction for visitors and an impressive display of the royal presence.

Rosenborg Palace, also in Copenhagen, is a magnificent Renaissance palace known for its impressive architecture and rich history. Originally built as the summer residence of King Christian IV, the castle is now home to the National Museum of Denmark, which houses an impressive collection of royal artwork, trinkets, and historical artifacts. The Crown Jewels and the Crown of the Kingdom of Denmark can be admired here.

Frederiksborg Castle, located in Hillerød, is a majestic Renaissance castle built by King Christian IV. It is considered one of the most beautiful castles in Europe and now serves as the Danish National Museum of History. The magnificent interior, impressive gardens and picturesque castle lake make Frederiksborg a popular destination for tourists and history lovers.

Christiansborg Palace, in Copenhagen, is a significant palace that plays an important role in Danish politics. It houses the Danish Parliament, the Supreme Court, and the Prime Minister's Office. The tower of the castle offers a breathtaking view over the city and the harbour area.

Kronborg Castle, also known as "Hamlet's Castle", is a UNESCO World Heritage Site and a historic landmark. It is located in Helsingør and played an important role in the trade and defense of the Öresund Strait. The connection to Shakespeare's drama "Hamlet" has immortalized the castle in literary history.

Denmark's royal castles are not only witnesses to royal splendour, but also places of historical significance and cultural richness. They are living monuments of the past that reflect Denmark's rich history. From the magnificent palaces in Copenhagen to the majestic Renaissance castles in the countryside, these castles tell the stories of the royal dynasty and the Danish people, while also being a source of admiration, education and inspiration for visitors from all over the world.

Denmark's contribution to the music world: from classical music to pop

Denmark's music scene has produced diverse talent throughout history and made impressive contributions to the global music landscape. From classical compositions to jazz to modern pop and electronic music, Denmark has exerted a rich and diverse musical influence.

Denmark's classical music tradition dates back to the 16th century, when composers such as Mogens Pederson created their first works. Over time, important Danish composers such as Carl Nielsen and Niels Gade have gained international recognition. Often referred to as the "father of Danish music", Carl Nielsen left behind a significant legacy of symphonies, chamber music and operas, known for their innovative harmony and melody.

In the world of jazz, Denmark has also exerted a remarkable influence. Founded in 1979, the Copenhagen Jazz Festival has become one of Europe's most important jazz events. Jazz musicians such as Ben Webster, Niels-Henning Ørsted Pedersen and Palle Mikkelborg have left their mark on the Danish jazz scene and achieved international fame.

In the field of pop music, Denmark has produced an impressive number of artists in recent decades who have gained worldwide recognition. Artists such as Aqua, known for their hit "Barbie Girl", and MØ, whose song "Lean On" was a worldwide chart hit, have brought Danish pop music into the global mainstream.

Particularly noteworthy is the Danish electropop scene, which has become increasingly popular in recent years. Artists such as Oh Land, Trentemøller and MØ have attracted international attention with their innovative soundscapes and electronic elements.

The Danish music world has also produced outstanding artists in the field of classical opera singing talents, including Aksel Schiøtz and Inga Nielsen. Her impressive voices and interpretations have left their mark on opera stages in Denmark and around the world.

In recent years, Denmark's electronic music scene has gained worldwide attention. Artists such as Kölsch, Kasper Bjørke and Rune Reilly Kölsch have established themselves in the electronic music landscape and performed on international stages.

Denmark's diverse musical contribution reflects the country's cultural dynamism. From classical music tradition to modern pop culture, from jazz legends to electronic innovators, Denmark's music scene has produced a wealth of talent that transcends the boundaries of genres and impresses the world with their creative expressions. The diversity and quality of Danish music have helped to enrich the country's cultural heritage and influence the international music world.

The importance of design in Danish culture

Danish design has gained an unmistakable reputation worldwide for its elegance, functionality and aesthetics. The deep roots of design in Danish culture reflect the country's national identity, innovation and creativity.

Danish design is more than just aesthetics. It is an expression of the philosophy of everyday life and quality of life. The idea of "form follows function" is at the heart of Danish design, where the function of a product is crucial to its design. This clear connection between form and function characterizes the design of furniture, tableware, textiles and many other everyday objects.

The golden age of Danish design is often associated with the works of Arne Jacobsen, Hans J. Wegner and Poul Henningsen. These outstanding designers have not only created furniture that is now considered iconic, but have also laid the foundation for the timeless and functional design that has made Denmark famous worldwide.

A significant feature of Danish design is the ability to combine tradition and innovation. While traditional craftsmanship and techniques continue to be valued, the design is constantly evolving to meet the demands of the modern world. This combination of heritage and progress gives Danish design its unique identity.

The Danish design philosophy extends not only to products, but also to architecture and urban design. Copenhagen, as the capital of design, shows the integration of modern architecture into a historic environment. The "New Danish Modernism" has left a lasting impression on the architectural world and has been internationally recognized as a pioneering approach to urban planning.

Danish design also has a strong connection to nature. Nature plays a significant role in Danish culture and is reflected in the design. Natural materials such as wood, stone and wool are often used in Danish products, which shows a close connection to the environment and sustainability.

Danish design culture is fostered through education and research. Design schools such as the Royal Danish Academy of Fine Arts provide a platform for aspiring designers to develop and refine their skills. The Research Institute of Design and Technology works to push the boundaries of design and find innovative solutions to global challenges.

Danish design is not only an aesthetic expression, but also a reflection of the values and way of life of Danish society. The importance of functionality, sustainability and aesthetics reflects the Danish philosophy of life. The global recognition of Danish design shows that it's not just about aesthetics, but about a deep-rooted cultural identity that brings the capacity for beauty and innovation to everyday life.

Hygge: The secret to Danish well-being

Hygge is a term that is deeply rooted in Danish culture and embodies a unique way of life aimed at coziness, community and well-being. The term cannot be directly translated into English, as it describes a comprehensive concept that refers to a mood, an atmosphere, and a way of life.

Hygge is a reaction to Denmark's long, dark winter months, when the days are short and the weather is often cold and grey. During this period, the pursuit of cosiness plays a central role in the Danish lifestyle. Candlelight, soft blankets and warm drinks are just some of the elements that help to create a hygge atmosphere.

However, the art of hygge goes beyond mere physical coziness. It's about creating moments of joy, togetherness and inner contentment. Hygge is closely linked to social interaction, whether it's meeting friends and family, sharing meals, or simple activities such as nature walks.

Hygge also has a close connection to nature and simplicity. The feeling of well-being is often enhanced by the beauty of nature, experiencing the seasons and being mindful of the little things in life. Deceleration and the conscious enjoyment of moments are essential components of the hygge lifestyle.

Food and drink also play an important role in hygge. Traditional Danish dishes such as "smørrebrød" (open sandwiches) or "hot toddy" (a hot alcoholic beverage) are often associated with hygge. Preparing meals together and sharing food creates an atmosphere of connection and well-being.

Hygge also has an impact on Danish interior design. Comfortable furniture, warm colours and natural materials create an ambience that conveys a feeling of security and relaxation. Candles play a prominent role in the design of hygge rooms, as they provide soft lighting and create a cozy atmosphere.

It's important to emphasize that hygge involves more than just external circumstances. It is a way of life that aims to promote inner well-being. The pursuit of happiness, relaxation and contentment in life's small moments is at the heart of the hygge approach.

The philosophy of hygge has gained a lot of attention not only in Denmark but also internationally. People all over the world have started to incorporate elements of hygge into their lifestyles to achieve a higher level of coziness and well-being. The Danish way of life, embodied by hygge, reminds us to find joy in the little things in life and to cherish the important moments of relaxation and togetherness.

The Art of Danish Craftsmanship: Glassblowing and Ceramics

Danish craftsmanship has a rich tradition that manifests itself in various art forms, including glassblowing and ceramics. These two disciplines have played an important role in Denmark's cultural heritage over the centuries and are still of great importance today.

The art of glassblowing has a long history in Denmark, dating back to the 17th century. The town of Holmegaard, known for its glassworks, was one of the first places in Denmark where glass was produced. Today, Holmegaard Glashütte is famous for its high-quality glass products and innovative design. Danish glassblowers are known for their ability to create elegant shapes and vibrant colors that are appreciated all over the world.

In recent decades, Danish glassblowing has experienced a renaissance, with many artists and craftsmen combining the traditions of the past with modern techniques and designs. Artists such as Per Lütken and Finn Lynggaard have created groundbreaking works that push the boundaries of traditional glassblowing and open up new avenues for creative design possibilities.

The Danish ceramic tradition is just as rich and diverse. From handmade pottery to contemporary ceramic objects, Danish ceramic art has given rise to a wide range of styles and techniques. The artists of the Royal Danish Porcelain Manufactory, such as the famous "Flora Danica" series, have helped to bring Danish ceramics to the international stage.

Particularly noteworthy is the Danish tradition of "Stelton design", created by the Stelton company. The company's mission is to produce functional and aesthetically pleasing household items, including cutlery, crockery, and thermoses. The minimalist design and high-quality materials have made the Stelton design synonymous with Danish craftsmanship.

Danish craftsmanship is promoted by creative workshops, design schools and artists' collectives. The School of Arts and Crafts in Kolding and the Royal Danish Academy of Fine Arts offer programs and workshops for aspiring artists and craftsmen to develop their skills and find their artistic voice.

The art of Danish craftsmanship, be it glassblowing or ceramics, is in line with the values of Danish culture. Functionality, aesthetics and high-quality craftsmanship are cornerstones of these traditions. The Danish artists and craftsmen use their talent and passion to create timeless works of art that reflect the culture and history of the country while pushing the boundaries of design and engineering.

The importance of cycling in Denmark

Cycling is extremely important in Denmark and shapes everyday life, culture and cities in the country. It is not only a means of transport, but also a symbol of sustainability, health and quality of life.

Denmark is often referred to as one of the most bike-friendly countries in the world, and for good reason. The bicycle is an integral part of the transport system, and many Danes use it as their preferred mode of transport for their daily activities. In cities such as Copenhagen, Aarhus and Odense, cycle paths and infrastructure are widespread and well-developed, making cycling safe and practical.

The importance of cycling in Denmark is closely linked to the pursuit of sustainability. The bicycle is an emission-free means of transport that helps to reduce the environmental impact of transport. This awareness of environmental protection and sustainability is reflected in Danish culture and has helped to promote the bicycle as an eco-friendly alternative.

The Danish government has also taken measures to support cycling. Investments in infrastructure, such as the development of cycle lanes and parking spaces, contribute to the safety and convenience of cyclists. In addition, campaigns are being carried out to promote cycling to encourage people to use bicycles more.

Cycling in Denmark is not only a means of transport, but also an expression of the active lifestyle of the population. Many Danes use bicycles not only to get to work or school, but also for leisure activities such as trips to the countryside or to explore the surrounding area. The bicycle allows people to move around in the fresh air, enjoy their surroundings and stay active.

In addition, cycling has a positive impact on the health of the population. Regular cycling promotes physical fitness, strengthens the cardiovascular system and helps reduce stress. Denmark has a culture of physical activity, and cycling is a natural extension of this way of life.

Cycling also has social and community aspects. Cycling brings people together, whether it's on bike paths, on joint tours or at cycling events. It promotes interaction and exchange between people and contributes to the formation of a strong community.

Overall, cycling in Denmark symbolizes much more than just a way of getting around. It embodies the values of sustainability, health and community. The high importance of cycling in Danish culture has contributed to it becoming an integral part of daily life, influencing the way people get around, experience their environment and promote their health.

Denmark's folk festivals and traditions

Denmark is rich in vibrant folk festivals and traditions that are deeply rooted in the country's culture and offer a glimpse into the heart of the Danish community. These festivals are not only occasions to celebrate, but also moments when people come together to celebrate their cultural identity and keep ancient customs alive.

One such festival is "Fastelavn", the Danish equivalent of Halloween or Carnival. This traditional festival takes place in February and is celebrated with costumes, masks, games and sweet treats. A highlight of Fastelavn is the "barrel knocking", in which a barrel filled with sweets is beaten blind to free the sweets. This festival has a long history and is popular in schools, communities and families alike.

Another important festival is "Sankt Hans Aften", the Danish version of St. John's Night or Midsummer Festival. On the eve of June 24, people gather on beaches, parks and squares to light bonfires together and watch the burning of a straw doll. This festival has both pagan and Christian roots and marks the longest day of the year.

The "Julefrokost" is a traditional Christmas dinner where friends, family members and colleagues come together to celebrate the holiday season. During this festival, rich dishes are served, including pickled herrings, meats, cheeses and breads. The Julefrokost is an expression of community and conviviality, where the focus is on being together and sharing food.

"Grundlovsdag" or Constitution Day, which is celebrated on 5 June, is an important national holiday in Denmark. This day celebrates the Danish Constitution of 1849, which forms the basis for the country's modern democratic society. It is an opportunity for political gatherings, speeches and discussions about democracy and civil rights.

Another fascinating celebration is "Halloween", which has gained popularity in Denmark in recent years. Although it's an imported tradition, the Danes have added their own touch by dressing up in costumes, carving pumpkins, and collecting sweets. Halloween today is a fun and convivial celebration that is celebrated by many families and communities.

These folk festivals and traditions reflect the diversity of Danish culture and are a reflection of the values and customs that shape Danish society. Not only do they offer opportunities to celebrate, but they also provide insights into the country's history, community, and lived culture. Preserving and celebrating these festivals is a way to strengthen Danes' identity and pride in their cultural heritage, while sharing joy and connectedness.

The Danish language: history and characteristics

The Danish language is a fascinating aspect of Danish culture and history. It belongs to the North Germanic language family and is closely related to other Scandinavian languages such as Swedish and Norwegian. The history of the Danish language goes back centuries and reflects the development of the country, its contacts with other cultures and the social changes.

The roots of the Danish language can be traced back to the Viking Age. The Vikings were seafaring warriors and traders who brought Denmark into contact with other parts of Europe. During this time, an early form of Danish emerged, which was characterized by the various influences and cultural exchanges. The Old Norse language, from which Danish evolved, was written in runes and has left its mark on the earliest written records.

Over time, Danish continued to evolve and absorb influences from other languages. During the Danish colonial period in the 16th and 17th centuries, Danish had contact with other cultures, which led to an exchange of words and expressions. German and Dutch, in particular, left their mark on the vocabulary and grammar of Danish.

An important milestone in the development of the Danish language was the Reformation in the 16th century. With the introduction of printing by Martin Luther and other reformers, the Bible was printed in Danish for the first time. This helped to standardize the Danish written language and contributed to the spread of the language throughout the Kingdom.

Over the centuries, the Danish written language has undergone various changes and reforms in order to adapt it to modern circumstances. An important reform was the so-called "Retskrivningsreform" of 1948, which simplified and modernized the spelling and grammar of Danish.

A characteristic feature of the Danish language is intonation and intonation. Danish is a so-called "tonal language" in which the meaning of a word can be changed by the pitch of the speech. This emphasis gives the language a special melody and contributes to intelligibility.

The Danish language also has some peculiarities in terms of grammar and vocabulary. The use of articles and pronouns can be complex, and there are various grammatical cases for nouns. Danish vocabulary is characterized by its clarity and precision, which sometimes results in long compound words that accurately express a certain meaning.

In modern times, Danish has also been influenced by other languages, especially English. Many English words have found their way into the Danish vocabulary, especially in the fields of technology, science and commerce.

The Danish language is a living expression of Danish culture and identity. It reflects the country's history, diversity and developments. The preservation and cultivation of the Danish language is of great importance to the Danes and contributes to the strengthening of their cultural identity.

Cultural Politeness and Etiquette

Cultural politeness and manners play a central role in the social fabric of Danish society. They reflect the values of consideration, respect and community that characterize social interaction in Denmark. Danes attach great importance to being polite and respectful to each other, whether in the family, at work or in public.

One of the most conspicuous manners in Denmark is the "you" culture. Unlike in many other countries, people in Denmark are often on first-name terms with each other at the first meeting. This reflects the egalitarian nature of Danish society, where hierarchies are dismantled and people meet on an equal footing.

Despite the casual "you" culture, politeness and respect are still of great importance. Danes are known to use polite phrases such as "Tak" (thank you) and "Undskyld" (excuse me) frequently. It is customary to maintain eye contact in public and show a friendly smile to signal friendliness and openness.

In Danish society, it is important to respect the privacy of others. You are expected to introduce yourself before entering into a conversation, and you should not interfere in private matters unless you are invited to do so. The Danes make it a point to keep an appropriate distance and not to be too intrusive.

Conviviality and a sense of community are also important aspects of cultural courtesy in Denmark. It is customary to receive hosts or guests at home and meet each other in an informal atmosphere. During these meetings, people often eat and drink together, and are expected to engage in lively conversations.

The Danish work culture also reflects the values of politeness and respect. It is customary for colleagues to be on a first-name basis and to create an informal atmosphere. At the same time, professionalism and efficiency are highly valued, and punctual attendance at meetings and appointments is expected.

Cultural politeness and manners in Denmark are deeply rooted in society and contribute to harmony and good cooperation. They are an expression of appreciation for the individuality and needs of other people and help to create a pleasant and respectful social environment. The balance between a relaxed "you" culture and respectful politeness makes Danish society unique and shapes everyday interaction in a positive way.

The role of religion in Danish society

The role of religion in Danish society is a fascinating and complex topic that reflects historical development, cultural changes and social norms. Denmark has a long religious history, shaped by different faiths and currents, and today's society reflects a mixture of tradition, secularity and pluralism.

Historically, Christianity has been the dominant religion in Denmark. In the 10th century, the country was Christianized, and Christianity remained an important cultural and religious force for centuries. The Danish People's Church, the Evangelical Lutheran state church of Denmark, plays a central role in the country's religious landscape. It is not only an institution of faith, but also a symbol of national identity and history.

Despite the historical connection to Christianity, Denmark today is a society with a high rate of secularity. Many people see themselves as secular or non-religious individuals, and religiosity has declined in recent decades. The Danes are known for their liberal attitude towards freedom of belief and religious diversity, and the separation of church and state is a fundamental principle of Danish society.

In addition to Christianity, there is a growing presence of other faiths in Denmark, especially Islam. Immigration from different countries has led to an increase in cultural diversity, which also brings with it religious diversity. Mosques and other religious institutions are present in cities and towns, and interreligious dialogue is gaining in importance.

The role of religion in Danish society is also evident in certain cultural traditions and holidays. Although Christmas and Easter are celebrated in a cultural context, they often have a secular meaning and are associated with family gatherings, gifts, and celebrations. Other religious festivals, such as the Muslim festival of sacrifice Eid al-Adha or the Jewish festival of lights Hanukkah, are celebrated by the respective communities.

Discussions about religion in Danish society often revolve around issues such as religious freedom, secularism, and cultural integration. The debate about the wearing of religious symbols in public or educational institutions is an example of how the balance between individual religious practice and the values of secular society is sought.

Overall, the role of religion in Danish society shows the complex relationship between faith, culture and social norms. Denmark is a country that is in a constant state of change, and the way religion is perceived and practiced reflects these changes. Danes pride themselves on being an open and inclusive society that respects religious freedom and integrates the different facets of faith in a modern context.

Educational system and intellectual traditions

The education system in Denmark is an integral part of society and reflects the high intellectual standards and appreciation for knowledge and education. The Danish educational tradition has a long history and is characterized by modern approaches, a wide range of educational opportunities and a strong focus on individual development and critical thinking.

The basis of the Danish education system is compulsory education, which includes children between the ages of 6 and 16. The primary school lays the foundation for the educational experience, emphasizing social skills, creativity and hands-on learning in addition to academic subjects. A distinctive feature of the Danish education system is the emphasis on students' independence and ownership, who are encouraged to pursue their interests and actively participate in the learning process.

After primary school, students have the opportunity to attend secondary schools that offer various specializations such as science, languages, arts or commerce. The Gymnasium prepares students for higher education and provides a broad knowledge as well as the ability to think critically and solve complex problems. The Danish education system emphasizes holistic development and promotes both intellectual and social skills.

Higher education in Denmark is characterized by its quality and openness. Universities and colleges offer a wide range of degree programs ranging from the humanities to the natural sciences and social sciences. The Danish higher education landscape attaches great importance to interdisciplinary research and practical applications. Some Danish universities are internationally renowned and attract students from all over the world.

Denmark's intellectual tradition spans centuries and has produced important thinkers and writers. Names such as Søren Kierkegaard, Hans Christian Andersen and Niels Bohr are internationally known and have left their mark on the country's intellectual heritage. Kierkegaard was an influential philosopher whose works influenced the understanding of existence, faith, and morality. Andersen was one of the most famous storytellers, whose stories continue to fascinate generations of children and adults to this day. Niels Bohr was a pioneer of quantum physics and contributed significantly to the development of modern physics.

The Danish intellectual tradition is also reflected in art, literature and science. Denmark has a rich literary history, ranging from classical works to contemporary authors. The arts are thriving in Denmark, and the country has a vibrant cultural scene with theaters, galleries, and music venues.

Overall, Denmark's education system is closely linked to the country's intellectual traditions. It emphasizes the importance of knowledge, critical thinking, and creative expression. Danish society attaches great importance to education as a tool for personal development and to strengthen the future of the country. Denmark's intellectual traditions have shaped the country and contribute to cultural diversity and innovation.

Denmark's social welfare policy

Denmark's social welfare policy is a pioneering model that is recognized worldwide. It has a profound effect on people's lives and shapes the social structure of the country. The Danish welfare system is based on the principles of social justice, equality and solidarity and aims to improve the quality of life of citizens, promote equal opportunities and strengthen social inclusion.

One of the foundations of Danish welfare policy is the principle of universal social benefits. This means that all citizens, regardless of their income or social status, are entitled to certain benefits. These include health care, education, childcare, and social support. This system helps to reduce social inequalities and ensure a basic level of prosperity and quality of life for all.

The Danish healthcare system is an example of efficiency and accessibility. Citizens have access to high-quality health care, and the costs are largely financed by taxes. Health insurance covers both inpatient and outpatient treatment, and waiting times are relatively short compared to other countries. Prevention and health promotion are also important aspects of the system.

Denmark's education system is another feature of social welfare policy. Education is free and accessible to all, from primary school to higher education. This contributes to the promotion of educational equity and the development of a highly skilled workforce. At the same time, emphasis is placed on lifelong learning in order to promote the professional development and adaptability of citizens.

Childcare in Denmark is also exemplary. Parents have the right to paid parental leave, and kindergartens and daycare centers provide high-quality care for preschoolers. This allows parents to better reconcile family and work and contributes to gender equality.

Denmark's labour market policy aims to promote employment and support social inclusion. Flexible working time models, unemployment benefits and training opportunities are instruments that help to reduce unemployment and integrate people into the labour market.

Danish welfare policy is not only focused on short-term support, but also on the long-term promotion of education, health and social participation. It creates a strong social bond and fosters a sense of community. Citizens feel supported and encouraged to reach their full potential, which in turn contributes to the country's economic stability and social prosperity. Overall, Denmark's social welfare policy is a model for other countries looking for sustainable and inclusive solutions to improve the lives of their citizens.

Sustainability and environmental protection in Denmark

Denmark is internationally known for its exemplary commitment to sustainability and environmental protection. The country has become a global leader in promoting environmentally friendly practices, using renewable energy, and finding innovative solutions to environmental challenges.

A central element of Denmark's sustainability strategy is the promotion of renewable energies. Denmark has set itself the ambitious goal of becoming completely climate-neutral by 2050. This goal will be achieved by investing in wind energy, solar energy and biomass. Denmark is one of the world's largest producers of wind energy and has a long tradition of using wind turbines to generate electricity. Offshore wind farms can be found on the coast and provide a significant portion of the country's electricity needs.

The Danish government has also taken measures to make the transport sector more sustainable. Cycling is a widespread and popular form of transportation in Denmark, which helps to reduce CO2 emissions. In addition, electric vehicles are being promoted and charging stations for electric cars are widespread in cities. Public transport is well developed and offers an environmentally friendly alternative to private transport.

Denmark has also developed innovative approaches in the field of waste management. The country relies on recycling and waste prevention to minimize the environmental impact. A deposit system for beverage packaging has helped to reduce the consumption of single-use bottles. In cities, waste separation and environmentally friendly disposal are practiced in order to conserve resources and protect the environment.

The preservation of the natural environment is another concern of Denmark. The country has a rich biodiversity and a diverse flora and fauna. National parks and nature reserves are protected and maintained to preserve biodiversity. The Wadden Sea, a UNESCO World Heritage Site, is an important habitat for numerous species of birds and marine life.

The Danish government and the population are also taking climate change seriously. Strategies for adapting to rising sea levels, changing weather conditions and natural disasters are being developed and implemented. Denmark is committed to ambitious climate targets internationally and is actively working on global efforts to reduce greenhouse gas emissions.

Overall, Denmark's commitment to sustainability and environmental protection shows that a responsible attitude towards nature and the environment plays a crucial role in shaping a future worth living. The country sets standards for environmental sustainability that have not only national but also international implications. Denmark proves that innovative approaches and collective efforts can help address environmental challenges and create a sustainable future.

Denmark's role in the EU and international relations

Denmark plays an important role in the European Union (EU) and in international relations. The country has established itself as an active and responsible actor on the global stage, advocating for a wide range of political, economic and social issues.

Denmark has been a member of the EU since 1973 and has played an important role in the decades of its membership. As a pro-European country, Denmark has participated in shaping EU policy and has been committed to strengthening European integration. It has been actively involved in the development of EU treaties and initiatives and is known for its constructive cooperation with other Member States.

However, Denmark's relationship with the EU is also characterised by a special dynamic. Denmark has distanced itself from EU policy in some areas, notably monetary union and the common defence policy. The country has decided not to adopt the euro and has an opt-out clause for security matters. This reflects a desire to preserve national sovereignty in certain areas, while reaping the benefits of EU membership.

In international relations, Denmark is committed to multilateral cooperation and diplomatic solutions. The country is a member of the United Nations (UN) and actively contributes to various UN programs and initiatives. Denmark is also involved in international conflict resolution processes and promotes human rights, peace and security.

Another important element in Denmark's international relations is its role as a donor of development aid. The country supports projects and programmes in developing countries to promote social and economic development, fight poverty and improve educational opportunities. Denmark is also committed to environmental protection and climate change adaptation in international contexts.

NATO (North Atlantic Treaty Organization) also plays an important role in Denmark's international relations. The country is a member of this military alliance and is committed to contributing to collective defense. Denmark has participated in various peacekeeping operations and humanitarian missions to contribute to stability and security in various regions.

Overall, Denmark's role in the EU and in international relations is characterised by commitment, cooperation and a balanced approach. The country is committed to common values, but at the same time upholding its national interests and sovereignty. Denmark is an active participant in global efforts to promote democracy, human rights, peace and sustainable development.

Art Galleries and Museums: Preserving Denmark's Cultural Heritage

Denmark is rich in cultural heritage and has a long tradition of promoting art and culture. Art galleries and museums play a crucial role in preserving and showcasing this heritage, and they are a showcase for the country's diverse history, art, and creativity.

Danish art galleries and museums offer a wide range of collections representing different eras, styles, and artists. The National Museum in Copenhagen is an outstanding example of an institution that comprehensively presents Denmark's cultural heritage. Here, visitors will find artifacts from the Viking Age, Renaissance, Baroque, and other historical periods. The museum offers insights into the history, culture and everyday life of centuries past.

The Danish capital, Copenhagen, is also home to some of Europe's most prestigious art museums. The Statens Museum for Kunst (National Gallery) presents an impressive collection of Danish and international works of art from antiquity to the present day. Here, visitors can admire masterpieces by artists such as Bertel Thorvaldsen, Vilhelm Hammershøi and Carl Bloch.

Modern art is also highly valued in Denmark. The Louisiana Museum of Modern Art, north of Copenhagen, is known for its extensive collection of contemporary artwork. The museum houses works by artists such as Pablo Picasso, Andy Warhol, Yoko Ono, and many others. It also features impressive exhibitions showcasing current art movements and creative ideas.

Unique museums that focus on specific topics can also be found in Denmark. The Vikingeskibsmuseet (Viking Ship Museum) in Roskilde displays reconstructed Viking ships and offers insights into the country's maritime history. The Hans Christian Andersen Museum in Odense tells the story of the famous Danish storyteller and author.

Denmark is proud of its cultural diversity and strives to preserve art and history for generations to come. Museums are often renovated and modernized to provide interactive exhibition areas and innovative presentation methods. Education and cultural participation are important goals, and many museums offer educational programs, tours, and events for visitors of all ages.

Overall, the art galleries and museums reflect Denmark's commitment to preserving and promoting its rich cultural heritage. They offer visitors the opportunity to immerse themselves in the country's history, art, and creativity, and to make a deeper connection to Danish identity.

A look into the future: challenges and opportunities for Denmark

Denmark's future faces a multitude of challenges and opportunities that will shape the country in the coming years. These factors are reflected in various areas and will influence the social, economic, political, and cultural landscape of the country.

One of the biggest challenges facing Denmark is climate change. Like many other nations, Denmark strives to reduce its greenhouse gas emissions and promote sustainable energy resources. The country has set itself the ambitious goal of being carbon neutral by 2050 and is investing heavily in renewable energy, electric mobility and green technologies. Protecting the environment and adapting to the effects of climate change will continue to play a key role. Demographic development is another important challenge. Denmark, like many other Western countries, is facing an aging population and a decline in the birth rate. This can have an impact on social systems, the world of work and economic dynamism. The government is implementing measures to promote family planning and support parents to address this trend. However, digitalization and technology development also offer numerous opportunities. Denmark has established itself as a pioneer in digital transformation, promoting the development of start-ups and innovative technologies. The country's digital infrastructure enables efficient communication, education, and business operations.

International cooperation and Denmark's role in the EU will continue to be important. Global challenges such as security, trade and health require transnational solutions. Denmark will work to leverage its position in international forums and strengthen its partnerships.

Cultural diversity and integration will also become more important. With growing globalization and migration, Denmark is facing cultural and social changes. The country will strive to create an inclusive society where people of different backgrounds can live and work together.

Overall, Denmark's future is marked by a mix of challenges and opportunities. The country will rise to the challenges ahead by building on its strengths in innovation, sustainability, education and social welfare. The ability to adapt and actively shape the future will be crucial to ensure the prosperity and well-being of Danish society.

Epilogue

With a view to Denmark's rich history, diverse culture and modern developments, we can conclude a fascinating journey through this multifaceted country. From the Vikings to the Renaissance to today's modern society, Denmark has undergone impressive development and continuously shaped its identity.

The landscape of Denmark, from the stunning coastline to the green hills and forests, reflects the Danes' connection to nature. The wildlife, national parks, and sustainability efforts exemplify the country's commitment to environmental protection.

Denmark's cultural importance is evident in its art, literature, music, and proud heritage preserved through museums, galleries, and historical sites. The Danish language, politeness and social welfare policies are hallmarks of a society that values community, education and equal opportunities.

Denmark's role in the international arena, whether in the EU, in diplomatic relations or in global efforts, reflects the country's commitment to peace, human rights and sustainable development.

While Denmark faces challenges such as climate change, demographic change and technological development, the country will use its capacity for adaptation and innovation to shape a prosperous future.

The unique blend of tradition and modernity, closeness to nature and the pursuit of progress make Denmark an inspiring country that is worth continuing to explore and appreciate. In this book, we have tried to shed light on the many aspects and facets of Denmark and give an insight into the wonders of this Nordic gem. The journey ends here, but Denmark's history and heritage will continue to arouse the curiosity and enthusiasm of explorers, travelers and culture lovers from all over the world.

Printed in Great Britain
by Amazon